# French

## Key Stage 2
## For ages 9-11

## Practise & Learn

Published by CGP

Editors:
Lucy Loveluck
Matteo Orsini Jones
Holly Poynton

CD contributors:
Chris Dennett
Anne-Laure Kenny
Sam Norman

With thanks to Florence Bonneau, Sandrine Moyle,
and Jennifer Underwood for the proofreading.

ISBN: 978 1 84762 987 6

With thanks to Jan Greenway for the copyright research.

Printed by Elanders Ltd, Newcastle upon Tyne
Clipart from Corel®

Based on the classic CGP style created by Richard Parsons.

# Contents

# Hello!
## Bonjour!

**Salut.**
Hi.

**Bonjour! Ça va?**
Hello! How are you?

**Assez bien. Et toi?**
Quite well. And you?

**Très bien, merci!**
Very well, thanks!

**Au revoir.**
Goodbye.

**Au revoir!**
Goodbye!

**bonsoir** good evening

**bonne nuit** good night

**à bientôt** see you soon

**ça va bien** I'm well

**bien** well

**pas très bien** not very well

Unscramble these French phrases.

n e i t
b t à ô

u n e t
n b i o n

n z e s
a s i e b

........ .................

............... .........

.............. ...........

Complete the conversation below in French.

**Bonsoir!**

.................................................

**Ça va?**

.................................................

**Au revoir!**

.................................................

You have been given some English words. These words have been spelt in French in the word search below. Find all the words.

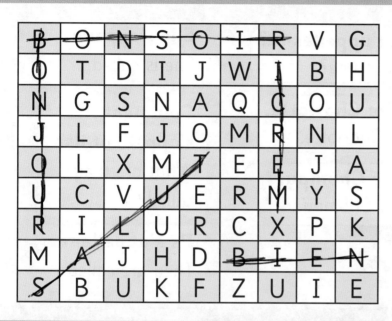

| B | O | N | S | O | I | R | V | G |
|---|---|---|---|---|---|---|---|---|
| O | T | D | I | J | W | I | B | H |
| N | G | S | N | A | Q | C | O | U |
| J | L | F | J | O | M | R | N | L |
| O | L | X | M | T | E | E | J | A |
| U | C | V | U | E | R | M | Y | S |
| R | I | L | U | R | C | X | P | K |
| M | A | J | H | D | B | I | E | N |
| S | B | U | K | F | Z | U | I | E |

good evening
thanks
well
hi
hello

Read the speech bubbles and answer the questions below.

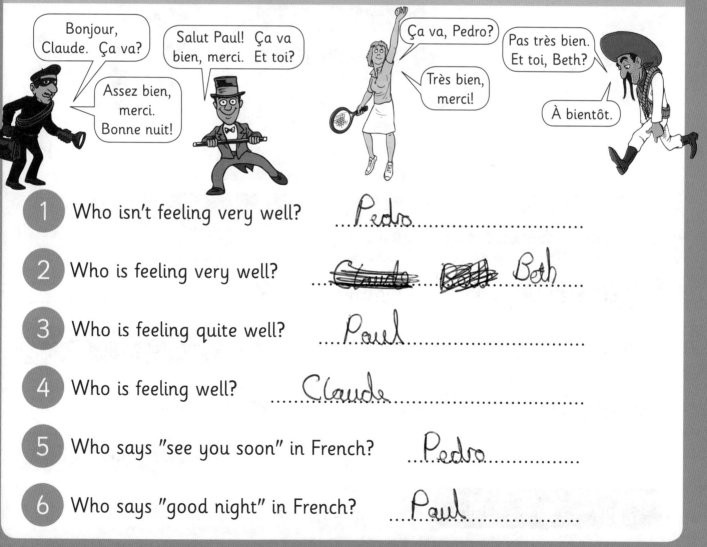

Bonjour, Claude. Ça va?

Salut Paul! Ça va bien, merci. Et toi?

Assez bien, merci. Bonne nuit!

Ça va, Pedro?

Très bien, merci!

Pas très bien. Et toi, Beth?

À bientôt.

1  Who isn't feeling very well? ...Pedro...

2  Who is feeling very well? ...Claude... Beth... Beth...

3  Who is feeling quite well? ...Paul...

4  Who is feeling well? ...Claude...

5  Who says "see you soon" in French? ...Pedro...

6  Who says "good night" in French? ...Paul...

5

s'appeller

Je m'appelle   il/elle s'appelle
tu t'appelles   nous nous appello...

# What is your name?

Comment t'appelles-tu?

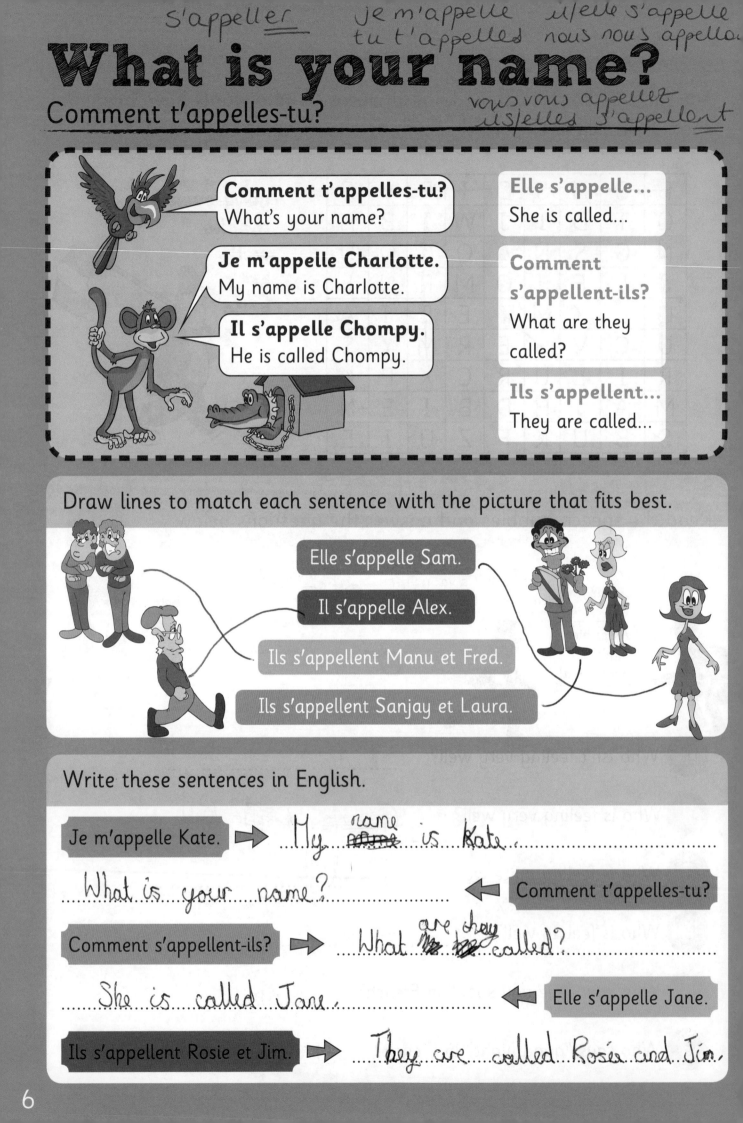

**Comment t'appelles-tu?**
What's your name?

**Je m'appelle Charlotte.**
My name is Charlotte.

**Il s'appelle Chompy.**
He is called Chompy.

**Elle s'appelle...**
She is called...

**Comment s'appellent-ils?**
What are they called?

**Ils s'appellent...**
They are called...

Draw lines to match each sentence with the picture that fits best.

Elle s'appelle Sam.

Il s'appelle Alex.

Ils s'appellent Manu et Fred.

Ils s'appellent Sanjay et Laura.

Write these sentences in English.

Je m'appelle Kate. ➡ My ~~name~~ is Kate.

What is your name? ⬅ Comment t'appelles-tu?

Comment s'appellent-ils? ➡ What ~~are they~~ called?

She is called Jane. ⬅ Elle s'appelle Jane.

Ils s'appellent Rosie et Jim. ➡ They are called Rosie and Jim.

6

Correct these sentences by crossing out the wrong words.

1 Je m'appelle / ~~m'appelles~~ Jo.

2 Il s'appelle / ~~s'appellent~~ Alf.

3 ~~Elle~~ / Il s'appelle David.

4 Ils ~~s'appelle~~ / s'appellent Harry et Nicolas.

5 Comment ~~s'appelle~~ / s'appellent -ils?

6 Comment ~~t'appelle-tu~~ / t'appelles-tu?

7 ~~Il~~ / Elle s'appelle Leanne.

Write a sentence in French for each of these pictures.

Jérôme

Il s'appelle Jérôme.

Julie

Elle s'appelle Julie

Valentin

Il s'appelle Valentin

Camille et James

Ils s'appellent Camille et James

Make three sentences in French using the words in the boxes.

m' | s' | Claude | s' | Paul | Guillaume | Ils

appelle | appelle | Elle | et | appellent | Je | Marie

1 Ils s'appellent Paul et ~~Ils~~ Claude.

2 Elle s'appelle Marie.

3 Je ~~m'appelle~~ m'appelle Guillaume.

7

# Numbers

## Les nombres

Here are the numbers from 1 to 30 in French.

| | | | |
|---|---|---|---|
| 1 **un** | 9 **neuf** | 17 **dix-sept** | 25 **vingt-cinq** |
| 2 **deux** | 10 **dix** | 18 **dix-huit** | 26 **vingt-six** |
| 3 **trois** | 11 **onze** | 19 **dix-neuf** | 27 **vingt-sept** |
| 4 **quatre** | 12 **douze** | 20 **vingt** | 28 **vingt-huit** |
| 5 **cinq** | 13 **treize** | 21 **vingt-et-un** | 29 **vingt-neuf** |
| 6 **six** | 14 **quatorze** | 22 **vingt-deux** | 30 **trente** |
| 7 **sept** | 15 **quinze** | 23 **vingt-trois** | |
| 8 **huit** | 16 **seize** | 24 **vingt-quatre** | |

Count how many items there are in each group.
Write the number in French in the box.

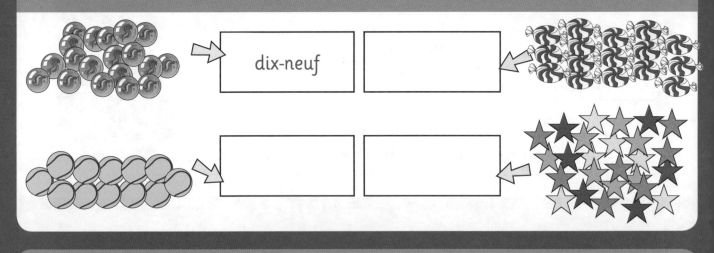

dix-neuf

Write the answers to these sums in French.

onze + douze =  vingt-trois

vingt-quatre − sept =

seize + cinq =

vingt-huit − dix =

trente − quinze =

dix-sept + huit =

**Quel âge as-tu?**
How old are you?

**Quel âge ont-ils?**
How old are they?

**Quel âge a-t-il?**
How old is he?

**Quel âge a-t-elle?**
How old is she?

**Ils ont trois ans.**
They are three years old.

**J'ai dix ans.**
I'm ten years old.

**Il a seize ans.**
He is sixteen years old.

**Elle a vingt-neuf ans.**
She is twenty-nine years old.

Match each question with a suitable answer, and write the age in the box.

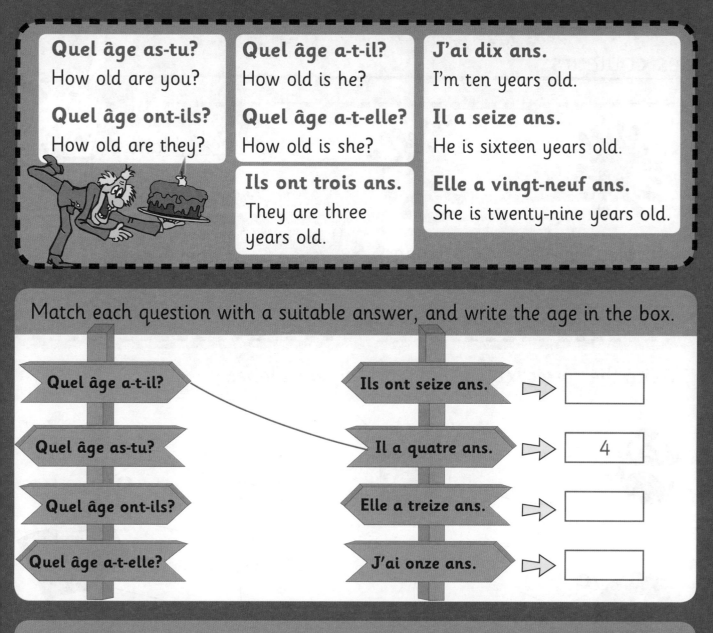

Quel âge a-t-il?

Quel âge as-tu?

Quel âge ont-ils?

Quel âge a-t-elle?

Ils ont seize ans. ➡ [ ]

Il a quatre ans. ➡ [ 4 ]

Elle a treize ans. ➡ [ ]

J'ai onze ans. ➡ [ ]

**Quel âge ont-ils?** Write how old each person is, in French.

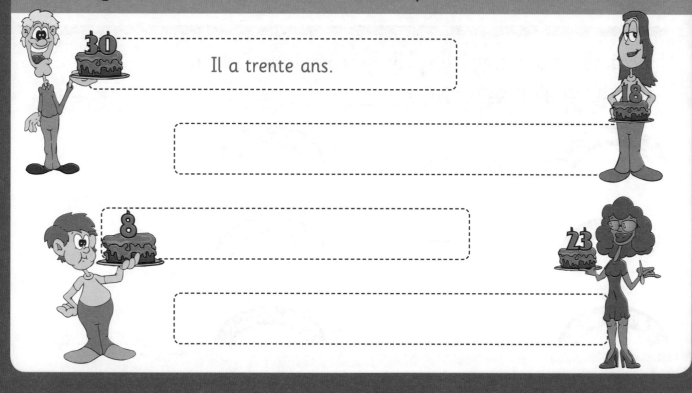

Il a trente ans.

# Colours

Les couleurs

rouge

vert

blanc

bleu

jaune

noir

Write the correct colour in French on each label.

Unscramble the letters to spell the colours in French.
Write the English next to them.

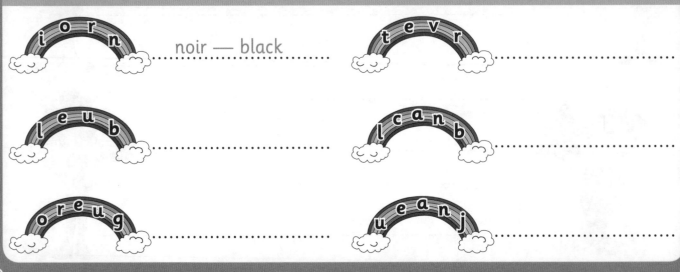

i o r n  ...... noir — black ......

t e v r  ...................................

l e u b  ...................................

l c a n b  ...................................

o r e u g  ...................................

u e a n j  ...................................

rose    orange

**Il est...** (masculine words)
He / It is...

**Elle est...** (feminine words)
She / It is...

violet    marron

Complete the crossword below with the French words.

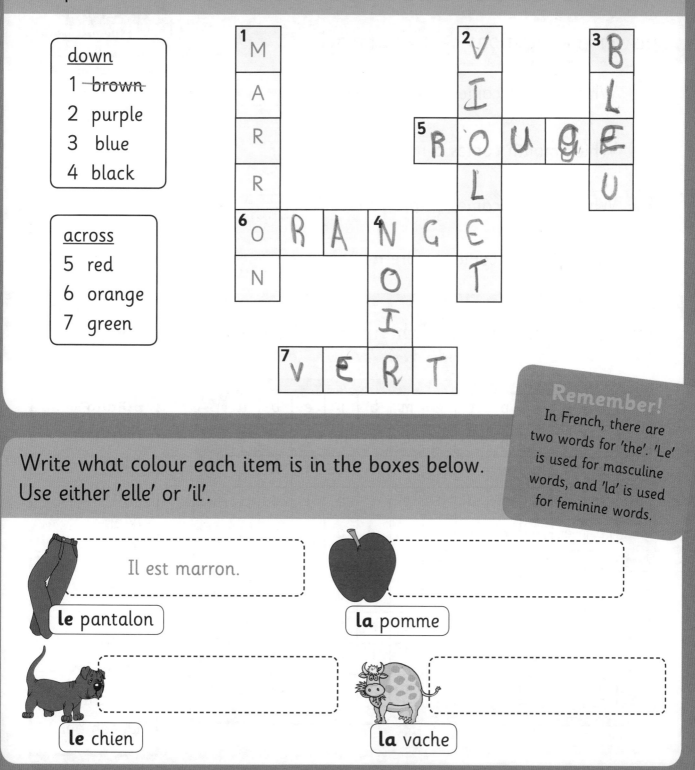

down
1 ~~brown~~
2 purple
3 blue
4 black

across
5 red
6 orange
7 green

<sup>1</sup>M A R R O N
<sup>2</sup>V I O L E T
<sup>3</sup>B L E U
<sup>5</sup>R O U G E
<sup>6</sup>O R A N G E
<sup>4</sup>N O I R
<sup>7</sup>V E R T

**Remember!**
In French, there are two words for 'the'. 'Le' is used for masculine words, and 'la' is used for feminine words.

Write what colour each item is in the boxes below.
Use either 'elle' or 'il'.

Il est marron.

**le** pantalon

**la** pomme

**le** chien

**la** vache

11

# Months

## Les mois

janvier — January
février — February
mars — March
avril — April
mai — May
juin — June
juillet — July
août — August
septembre — September
octobre — October
novembre — November
décembre — December

**Remember!**
In French, the first letters of months are lower case.

Answer the questions below in French.

① Which month comes after **mars**? ..............................

② Which month comes 3 months after **juin**? ...........................................

③ Which month comes before **janvier**? ...............................................

④ Which month comes before **août**? ..........................................................

Find the French months of the year in the word search below.

| o | s | e | p | t | e | m | b | r | e | b | a |
|---|---|---|---|---|---|---|---|---|---|---|---|
| c | e | d | h | d | é | c | e | m | b | r | e |
| t | û | a | w | j | c | i | s | t | f | n | g |
| o | p | o | m | u | l | é | l | b | i | o | f |
| b | é | û | c | i | d | e | m | a | i | v | é |
| r | d | t | g | n | a | e | a | a | j | e | v |
| e | c | f | a | j | h | b | r | û | d | m | r |
| e | a | v | r | i | l | d | s | k | s | b | i |
| é | b | k | j | u | i | l | l | e | t | r | e |
| j | a | n | v | i | e | r | n | s | o | e | r |

January
February
March
April
May
June
July
August
September
October
November
December

**Quelle est la date de ton anniversaire?**
When is your birthday?

**C'est le dix mai.**
It's the 10th of May.

## Write when each chef's birthday is, in French.

6th May → C'est le six mai.

18th September ←

2nd June →

26th February ←

## Write these sentences in English.

**Remember!**
If the date is the first of the month, you say 'le premier', e.g. 'C'est le premier août', which means 'It's the first of August'.

1 C'est le vingt-trois mars. It's the 23rd of March.

2 C'est le trente novembre. ...................................................

3 C'est le douze juillet. ...................................................

4 C'est le quatre août. ...................................................

5 C'est le premier avril. ...................................................

## Answer the question below, in French.

Quelle est la date de ton anniversaire?

13

# My family
## Ma famille

**Remember!**
The word for 'my' changes. If the following word is feminine, use 'ma', and if the word is masculine, use 'mon'.

**ma mère** my mother

**mon père** my father

**mon grand-père** my grandfather

**moi** me

**mon beau-père** My stepfather

**Ma belle-mère** My stepmother

**ma grand-mère** my grandmother

**ma sœur** my sister

**mon frère** my brother

Read the text and answer the questions in English.

Ma mère s'appelle Belinda et mon père s'appelle Geoffrey.  Mon beau-père s'appelle Lloyd et ma grand-mère s'appelle Rita.  Ma sœur s'appelle Emily et elle a quinze ans.  Mon frère s'appelle Lucas et il a vingt ans.

1 What is Élodie's mother called?  Belinda

2 How old is Élodie's brother?

3 Who is Lloyd?

4 How old is Élodie's sister?

5 What is Élodie's father called?

6 Who is Rita?

Élodie

7 What is Élodie's sister called?

**Tu as des frères ou des sœurs?**
Do you have any brothers or sisters?

**Oui, j'ai un frère et une sœur.**
Yes, I have a brother and a sister.

**Non, je suis fils unique.**
No, I'm an only child (boy).

**Non, je suis fille unique.**
No, I'm an only child (girl).

**Remember!**
If you're talking about more than one brother or sister, add an 's', e.g. 'deux frères.'

## Write these sentences in French.

1  Do you have any brothers or sisters?

..................................................................

..................................................................

2  Yes, I have two sisters and a brother.

..................................................................

..................................................................

3  My name is Adam and I'm an only child.

..................................................................

..................................................................

**Tu as des frères ou des sœurs?**  Fill in each person's answer in French.

# Animals

## Les animaux

### Remember!
L'oiseau is a masculine word and l'araignée is feminine. When words begin with a vowel, the 'le' or 'la' becomes 'l'.

le chien   le cheval   le lapin   l'oiseau   la souris   le chat

le hamster   le poisson   le serpent   l'araignée   la tortue

Unscramble the letters to spell the names of some animals in French. Don't forget to include either **'la'**, **'le'** or **'l'**.

é a a l' g e n r i ⇒ .............  ..............................

.............  .............................. ⇐ i e h c e l n

s n o i p s e l o ⇒ .............  ..............................

.............  .............................. ⇐ s l e e t r e n p

Write the correct French word for each picture below.

# Practise and Learn

# French
# Ages 9-11

# Answers

This section shows each of the pages from the book with the answers filled out.

The pages are laid out in the same way as the book itself, so the questions can be easily marked by you, or by your child.

There are also helpful learning tips with some of the pages.

---

**4**

## Hello!
Bonjour!

> **Salut.**
> Hi.

> **Bonjour! Ça va?**
> Hello! How are you?

> **Assez bien. Et toi?**
> Quite well. And you?

> **Très bien, merci!**
> Very well, thanks!

> **Au revoir.**
> Goodbye.

> **Au revoir!**
> Goodbye!

| | |
|---|---|
| bonsoir good evening | ça va bien I'm well |
| bonne nuit good night | bien well |
| à bientôt see you soon | pas très bien not very well |

**Unscramble these French phrases.**

n e i t
b t à ô

à    bientôt

u n e t
n b i o n

bonne    nuit

n z e s
a s i e b

assez    bien

**Complete the conversation below in French.**

> **Bonsoir!**

> **Ça va?**

> **Au revoir!**

VARIOUS ANSWERS POSSIBLE

Bonsoir!

Très bien, merci.

À bientôt!

4

---

**5**

You have been given some English words. These words have been spelt in French in the word search below. Find all the words.

| B | O | N | S | O | I | R | V | G |
|---|---|---|---|---|---|---|---|---|
| O | T | D | I | J | W | I | B | H |
| N | G | S | N | A | Q | C | O | U |
| J | L | F | J | O | M | R | N | L |
| O | L | X | M | T | E | E | J | A |
| U | C | V | U | E | R | M | Y | S |
| R | I | L | U | R | C | X | P | K |
| M | A | J | H | D | B | I | E | N |
| S | B | U | K | F | Z | U | I | E |

good evening
thanks
well
hi
hello

**Read the speech bubbles and answer the questions below.**

> Bonjour, Claude. Ça va?

> Assez bien, merci. Bonne nuit!

> Salut Paul! Ça va bien, merci. Et toi?

> Ça va, Pedro?

> Très bien, merci!

> Pas très bien. Et toi, Beth?

> À bientôt.

1. Who isn't feeling very well?    Pedro

2. Who is feeling very well?    Beth

3. Who is feeling quite well?    Paul

4. Who is feeling well?    Claude

5. Who says "see you soon" in French?    Pedro

6. Who says "good night" in French?    Paul

5

# What is your name?

## Comment t'appelles-tu?

**Comment t'appelles-tu?**
What's your name?

**Je m'appelle Charlotte.**
My name is Charlotte.

**Il s'appelle Chompy.**
He is called Chompy.

Elle s'appelle...
She is called...

Comment s'appellent-ils?
What are they called?

Ils s'appellent...
They are called...

Draw lines to match each sentence with the picture that fits best.

Elle s'appelle Sam.

Il s'appelle Alex.

Ils s'appellent Manu et Fred.

Ils s'appellent Sanjay et Laura.

Write these sentences in English.

Je m'appelle Kate. ➡ My name is Kate.

What is your name? ⬅ Comment t'appelles-tu?

Comment s'appellent-ils? ➡ What are they called?

She is called Jane. ⬅ Elle s'appelle Jane.

Ils s'appellent Rosie et Jim. ➡ They are called Rosie and Jim.

Correct these sentences by crossing out the wrong words.

1. Je m'appelle / ~~m'appelles~~ Jo.
2. Il s'appelle / ~~s'appellent~~ Alf.
3. ~~Elle~~ / Il s'appelle David.
4. Ils ~~s'appelle~~ / s'appellent Harry et Nicolas.
5. Comment ~~s'appelle~~ / s'appellent -ils?
6. Comment ~~t'appelle-tu~~ / t'appelles-tu?
7. ~~Il~~ / Elle s'appelle Leanne.

Write a sentence in French for each of these pictures.

Il s'appelle Jérôme.
Jérôme

Elle s'appelle Julie.
Julie

Il s'appelle Valentin.
Valentin

Ils s'appellent Camille et James.
Camille et James

Make three sentences in French using the words in the boxes.

m'  s'  Claude  s'  Paul  Guillaume  Ils
appelle  appelle  Elle  et  appellent  Je  Marie

1. Elle s'appelle Marie.
2. Ils s'appellent Paul et Guillaume. [VARIOUS ANSWERS POSSIBLE]
3. Je m'appelle Claude.

# Numbers

## Les nombres

Here are the numbers from 1 to 30 in French.

| | | | |
|---|---|---|---|
| 1 un | 9 neuf | 17 dix-sept | 25 vingt-cinq |
| 2 deux | 10 dix | 18 dix-huit | 26 vingt-six |
| 3 trois | 11 onze | 19 dix-neuf | 27 vingt-sept |
| 4 quatre | 12 douze | 20 vingt | 28 vingt-huit |
| 5 cinq | 13 treize | 21 vingt-et-un | 29 vingt-neuf |
| 6 six | 14 quatorze | 22 vingt-deux | 30 trente |
| 7 sept | 15 quinze | 23 vingt-trois | |
| 8 huit | 16 seize | 24 vingt-quatre | |

Count how many items there are in each group.
Write the number in French in the box.

dix-neuf    seize

douze    vingt-six

Write the answers to these sums in French.

onze + douze = vingt-trois    vingt-quatre − sept = dix-sept

seize + cinq = vingt-et-un    vingt-huit − dix = dix-huit

trente − quinze = quinze    dix-sept + huit = vingt-cinq

Quel âge as-tu?
How old are you?

Quel âge ont-ils?
How old are they?

Quel âge a-t-il?
How old is he?

Quel âge a-t-elle?
How old is she?

J'ai dix ans.
I'm ten years old.

Il a seize ans.
He is sixteen years old.

Ils ont trois ans.
They are three years old.

Elle a vingt-neuf ans.
She is twenty-nine years old.

Match each question with a suitable answer, and write the age in the box.

Quel âge a-t-il?    Ils ont seize ans. ⇨ 16

Quel âge as-tu?    Il a quatre ans. ⇨ 4

Quel âge ont-ils?    Elle a treize ans. ⇨ 13

Quel âge a-t-elle?    J'ai onze ans. ⇨ 11

**Quel âge ont-ils?** Write how old each person is, in French.

Il a trente ans.

Elle a dix-huit ans.

Il a huit ans.

Elle a vingt-trois ans.

If your child finds the final exercise on page 8 tricky, it might be helpful for them to work out the sums in English before translating their answers into French.

## 10 Colours
Les couleurs

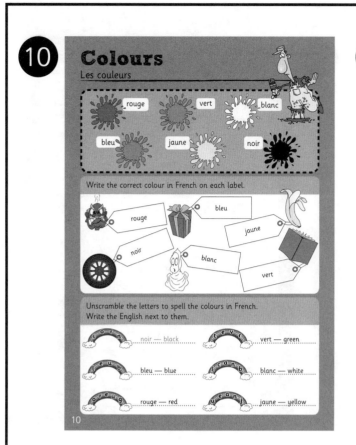

rouge | vert | blanc
bleu | jaune | noir

**Write the correct colour in French on each label.**

rouge | bleu
noir | jaune
blanc
vert

**Unscramble the letters to spell the colours in French. Write the English next to them.**

noir — black
vert — green
bleu — blue
blanc — white
rouge — red
jaune — yellow

10

## 11

_rose | _orange
violet | marron

Il est... (masculine words)
He / It is...
Elle est... (feminine words)
She / It is...

**Complete the crossword below with the French words.**

down
1 brown
2 purple
3 blue
4 black

across
5 red
6 orange
7 green

```
      1M        2V    3B
      A         I     L
      R    5R O U G E E
      R         L     U
    6O R A 4N G E
      N       O T
              I
          7V E R T
```

**Write what colour each item is in the boxes below. Use either 'elle' or 'il'.**

Il est marron. — **le** pantalon
Elle est rouge. — **la** pomme
Il est bleu. — **le** chien
Elle est rose. — **la** vache

11

For extra practice, ask your child to point to items around the house and say what colour they are in French.

## 12 Months
Les mois

janvier / January | février / February | mars / March | avril / April | mai / May | juin / June | juillet / July
août / August | septembre / September | octobre / October | novembre / November | décembre / December

**Answer the questions below in French.**

① Which month comes after **mars**? avril

② Which month comes 3 months after **juin**? septembre

③ Which month comes before **janvier**? décembre

④ Which month comes before **août**? juillet

**Find the French months of the year in the word search below.**

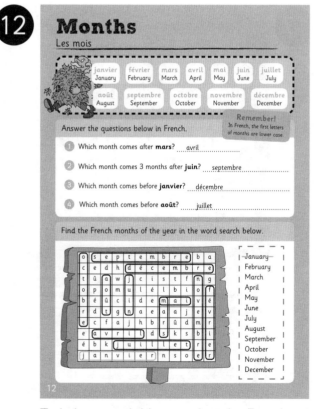

January
February
March
April
May
June
July
August
September
October
November
December

12

To help your child remember the French months, you could write them alongside the English words on a calendar or timetable.

## 13

Quelle est la date de ton anniversaire?
When is your birthday?

C'est le dix mai.
It's the 10th of May.

**Write when each chef's birthday is, in French.**

C'est le six mai — 6th May
C'est le dix-huit septembre. — 18th September
C'est le deux juin. — 2nd June
C'est le vingt-six février. — 26th February

**Write these sentences in English.**

① C'est le vingt-trois mars. It's the 23rd of March.

② C'est le trente novembre. It's the 30th of November.

③ C'est le douze juillet. It's the 12th of July.

④ C'est le quatre août. It's the 4th of August.

⑤ C'est le premier avril. It's the 1st of April.

**Answer the question below, in French.**

VARIOUS ANSWERS POSSIBLE

Quelle est la date de ton anniversaire?

C'est le deux janvier.

13

# My family
## Ma famille

ma mère — my mother
mon père — my father
mon grand-père — my grandfather
Mon beau-père — My stepfather
moi — me
Ma belle-mère — My stepmother
ma grand-mère — my grandmother
ma sœur — my sister
mon frère — my brother

**Remember!**
The word for 'my' changes. If the following word is feminine, use 'ma', and if the word is masculine, use 'mon'.

Read the text and answer the questions in English.

Ma mère s'appelle Belinda et mon père s'appelle Geoffrey. Mon beau-père s'appelle Lloyd et ma grand-mère s'appelle Rita. Ma sœur s'appelle Emily et elle a quinze ans. Mon frère s'appelle Lucas et il a vingt ans.

1 What is Élodie's mother called? Belinda

2 How old is Élodie's brother? 20 years old

3 Who is Lloyd? Élodie's stepfather

4 How old is Élodie's sister? 15 years old

5 What is Élodie's father called? Geoffrey

6 Who is Rita? Élodie's grandmother

7 What is Élodie's sister called? Emily

Élodie

14

---

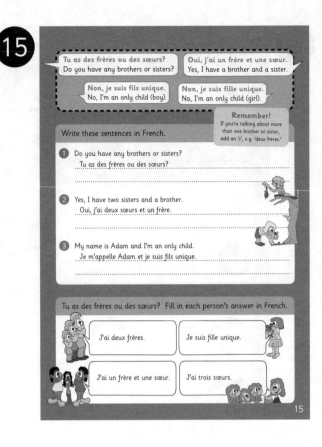

Tu as des frères ou des sœurs?
Do you have any brothers or sisters?

Oui, j'ai un frère et une sœur.
Yes, I have a brother and a sister.

Non, je suis fils unique.
No, I'm an only child (boy).

Non, je suis fille unique.
No, I'm an only child (girl).

**Remember!**
If you're talking about more than one brother or sister, add an 's', e.g. 'deux frères.'

Write these sentences in French.

1 Do you have any brothers or sisters?
Tu as des frères ou des sœurs?

2 Yes, I have two sisters and a brother.
Oui, j'ai deux sœurs et un frère.

3 My name is Adam and I'm an only child.
Je m'appelle Adam et je suis fils unique.

Tu as des frères ou des sœurs? Fill in each person's answer in French.

J'ai deux frères.

Je suis fille unique.

J'ai un frère et une sœur.

J'ai trois sœurs.

15

---

If your child finds the exercise on page 14 a bit tricky, it may be helpful for them to translate the speech bubble into English before they answer the questions.

---

# Animals
## Les animaux

**Remember!**
L'oiseau is a masculine word and l'araignée is feminine. When words begin with a vowel, the 'le' or 'la' becomes 'l'.

le chien, le cheval, le lapin, l'oiseau, la souris, le chat
le hamster, le poisson, le serpent, l'araignée, la tortue

Unscramble the letters to spell the names of some animals in French. Don't forget to include either 'la', 'le' or 'l''.

é a a l' g e n r i ⇒ l' araignée

le chien ⇐ i e h c e l n

s n o i p s e l o ⇒ le poisson

le serpent ⇐ s l e e t r e n p

Write the correct French word for each picture below.

la tortue

l'oiseau

le lapin

le cheval

16

---

As-tu un animal?
Do you have a pet?

Oui, j'ai...
Yes, I have...

Non, je n'ai pas d'animaux.
No, I don't have any pets.

Read the text and answer the questions in English.

J'ai trois chiens et un chat. Mon chat s'appelle Scruffy et il a deux ans. J'ai quatre lapins et trois araignées.

Karim

1 How many dogs does Karim have? three

2 Karim owns six spiders. True or false? false

3 Who is Scruffy? Karim's cat

4 How old is Scruffy? two years old

5 What pet does Karim have four of? rabbits

Your French penpal has sent you an email asking 'As-tu un animal?'. Write your answer below. Give lots of details about your animals.

Email
To: aristidep02@speedymail.fr
Subject: Les animaux

VARIOUS ANSWERS POSSIBLE

Oui, j'ai un cheval et une tortue.

Mon cheval s'appelle Muffin et il a sept ans.

Ma tortue s'appelle Shelly et elle a trente ans.

17

## 18. Clothes

Les vêtements

le jean · la chemise · le pantalon · le pull · la jupe
le tee-shirt · les chaussettes · les chaussures · la robe
le chapeau · les gants

**Je porte...** I am wearing...

Write the English next to each French word.

| | | | |
|---|---|---|---|
| le pantalon | (the) trousers | la jupe | (the) skirt |
| les gants | (the) gloves | la robe | (the) dress |
| la chemise | (the) shirt | le jean | (the) jeans |

Write a sentence in French to say what these characters are wearing.

Je porte un chapeau.

Je porte des chaussures.

Je porte des chaussettes.

Je porte un pull.

## 19

Il porte... He is wearing...

Elle porte... She is wearing...

Circle the sentence that describes each picture best.

Il porte une chemise jaune. *(circled)*
Il porte un chapeau bleu.
Il porte un pull marron.

Elle porte un pantalon rouge.
Il porte une chemise orange.
Il porte un pantalon rouge. *(circled)*

Elle porte une jupe jaune.
Elle porte une robe marron.
Elle porte une robe rose. *(circled)*

Elle porte une robe rose.
Elle porte un tee-shirt rose. *(circled)*
Elle porte un jean rose.

Read the text and answer the questions in English.

Maurice:
Je porte un chapeau vert, une chemise jaune et un pantalon bleu. Mon frère s'appelle Clément. Il porte un pull marron et un jean bleu. Ma sœur s'appelle Ella. Elle porte une jupe orange et un tee-shirt violet.

1. Who is wearing a brown jumper?    Clément / Maurice's brother
2. What colour are Maurice's trousers?    blue
3. Who is wearing a purple T-shirt?    Ella / Maurice's sister
4. Who is wearing blue jeans?    Clément / Maurice's brother
5. What colour is Ella's skirt?    orange

As an extension you could ask your child to write about what they are wearing, and what their friends are wearing, in French.

## 20. Food

La nourriture

le pain · les frites · le sandwich · le jambon · le fromage
la pomme · le chocolat · la pizza · les spaghettis · le yaourt

**Je mange...** I'm eating...

**Je voudrais...** I would like...

Unscramble these French words.

e f g e l m r a o → le fromage

j m e l n b o a → le jambon

l u e t y o r a → le yaourt

For each picture, write a sentence to say what you would like.

Je voudrais trois pommes.

Je voudrais quatre yaourts.

Je voudrais un sandwich.

## 21

la fourchette the fork
le couteau the knife
la cuillère the spoon
l'assiette the plate

**Peux-tu me passer le couteau, s'il te plaît?** Can you pass me the knife, please?

Draw lines to match the pictures to the French words.

l'assiette · le couteau · la fourchette · la cuillère

Write these sentences in English.

1. Peux-tu me passer la fourchette, s'il te plaît?
   Can you pass me the fork, please?

2. Je mange du chocolat.
   I'm eating (some) chocolate / I eat chocolate.

3. Peux-tu me passer la cuillère?
   Can you pass me the spoon?

4. Je voudrais une assiette.
   I would like a plate.

Practise asking 'Peux-tu me passer ... s'il te plaît?' with your child at the dinner table to help them learn the food vocabulary.

## What do you like doing?
Qu'est-ce que tu aimes faire?

| J'aime... | Je n'aime pas... |
|---|---|
| I like... | I don't like... |

...jouer au foot — ...playing football
...danser — ...dancing
...nager — ...swimming
...jouer du piano — ...playing the piano
...regarder la télé — ...watching TV
...écouter de la musique — ...listening to music
...lire — ...reading

Write these sentences in English.

J'aime regarder la télé. ➡ I like watching TV.

I don't like dancing. ⬅ Je n'aime pas danser.

J'aime jouer au foot. ➡ I like playing football.

I don't like swimming. ⬅ Je n'aime pas nager.

Write what each person likes or dislikes doing, in French.

Je n'aime pas lire.

J'aime écouter de la musique.

J'aime nager.

Je n'aime pas jouer du piano.

| Pourquoi? | C'est fantastique. | C'est nul. |
|---|---|---|
| Why? | It's fantastic. | It's rubbish. |
| Parce que... | C'est intéressant. | C'est ennuyeux. |
| Because... | It's interesting. | It's boring. |

Read the letter and answer the questions in English.

1 Name two things that Agnès likes doing.
  reading and playing football

2 What does Agnès say is fantastic?
  playing football

3 What does Agnès say is boring?
  dancing

4 What does Agnès say is rubbish?
  watching TV

5 What does Agnès say is interesting?
  reading

> J'aime lire, parce que c'est intéressant. J'aime jouer au foot, parce que c'est fantastique. Je n'aime pas regarder la télé, parce que c'est nul. Je n'aime pas danser, parce que c'est ennuyeux.
>
> Agnès

Answer the questions below in French.  VARIOUS ANSWERS POSSIBLE

Qu'est-ce que tu aimes faire? Pourquoi?

J'aime regarder la télé, parce que c'est intéressant.

If your child finds the letter exercise on page 23 tricky, they could translate the letter into English before answering the questions.

## What time is it?
Quelle heure est-il?

| Quelle heure est-il? | À dix heures... | ...du matin |
|---|---|---|
| What time is it? | At ten o'clock... | ...in the morning |
| Il est deux heures... | | ...du soir |
| It's two o'clock... | | ...in the evening |

For each picture below, write down what time it is in French.

Il est une heure.

Il est cinq heures.

Il est neuf heures.

Monique has written down what she likes doing on a Saturday. Answer the questions about her routine in English.

À dix heures du matin, je joue au foot.

À onze heures du matin, je regarde la télé.

À deux heures, je danse.

À six heures du soir, je joue du piano.

À huit heures du soir, j'écoute de la musique.

When does Monique like to dance?
  2 o'clock

What does Monique like to do at 11 am?
  watch TV

When does Monique like to play the piano?
  6 pm

What does Monique like to do at 8 pm?
  listen to music

Il est dix heures...
...et quart.
It's quarter past ten.
...et demie.
It's half past ten.

Il est midi.
It's midday.
Il est minuit.
It's midnight.

Draw the correct times onto these clocks.

Il est huit heures et quart.
Il est onze heures et demie.
Il est minuit.
Il est trois heures et demie.

Read the question below and give your answer in French.

Quelle heure est-il?   VARIOUS ANSWERS POSSIBLE
Il est quatre heures et demie.

Rewrite these sentences in French.

**Remember!**
Use the words from page 22 to help you answer these questions. In French, words like 'nager' can mean 'to swim' as well as 'swimming'.

1 At midday I like to swim.
  À midi j'aime nager.

2 At three o'clock I like to play football.
  À trois heures j'aime jouer au foot.

3 At quarter past six in the evening I like to dance.
  À six heures et quart du soir j'aime danser.

It might be useful for your child to look back at the 'Numbers' vocabulary (page 8) before trying these exercises.

## 26 The weather
Le temps

| Il fait... | ...beau. ...nice weather. | ...froid. ...cold. |
| It is... | ...mauvais. ...bad weather. | ...chaud. ...hot. |

| Il y a du soleil. It is sunny. | Il neige. It is snowing. | Il pleut. It is raining. |
| Il y a du vent. It is windy. | | |

Match each French phrase to the correct English phrase.

Il fait beau.　It's cold.　It's hot.　Il fait froid.

It's bad weather.　Il neige.　It's nice weather.

Il fait chaud.　It's snowing.　Il fait mauvais.

Fill in the blanks below to form phrases in French.

Il y a du soleil

Il y a du vent

Il pleut　Il neige

26

---

## 27

Read the question below and give your answer in French.

Quel temps fait-il aujourd'hui?

VARIOUS ANSWERS POSSIBLE
Il fait beau, il y a du soleil.

Write these sentences in French.

1　It is bad weather.　Il fait mauvais.

2　It is cold.　Il fait froid.

3　It is hot.　Il fait chaud.

Claude kept a weather diary for his week in France. Use it to answer the questions below in English.

| Mon | Aujourd'hui il fait beau. |
| Tue | Aujourd'hui il fait froid et il pleut. |
| Wed | Aujourd'hui il fait beau. |
| Thu | Aujourd'hui il fait chaud et il y a du vent. |
| Fri | Aujourd'hui il neige. |
| Sat | Aujourd'hui il neige et il y a du vent. |

What was the weather like on Monday?
The weather was nice.

Did it rain on Friday?
No

What was the weather like on Tuesday?
It was cold and it was raining.

On which days did it snow?
Friday and Saturday

27

To extend this exercise, your child could keep their own weather diary, in French.

---

## 28 In my town
Dans ma ville

| l'école school | le café coffee shop | les magasins shops | la bibliothèque library |
| la piscine swimming pool | le restaurant restaurant | la gare train station | la poste post office |

Dans ma ville, il y a...　In my town, there is / are...

Unscramble these French words.

e s l a p t o　　　e i i p l c s n a　　　l r u n a e r s t a e t

la　poste　　　la　piscine　　　le　restaurant

Remember!
'Il y a' means 'there is' or 'there are'.

Answer the questions below in English.

Dans ma ville, il y a une gare, une poste, un café, deux écoles, trois piscines, une bibliothèque et des magasins.

Leila

1　Is there a restaurant in Leila's town?　no

2　How many coffee shops are there?　one

3　How many swimming pools are there?　three

4　How many schools are there?　two

5　Is there a library in Leila's town?　yes

28

---

## 29

Answer the questions below in English.

Remember!
In French, 'de le' becomes 'du'. So you say 'en face du restaurant', not 'en face de le restaurant'.

La piscine est à côté de la poste. La gare est en face de la poste et près du café.

Le café est à côté de la gare et en face de l'école. La poste est en face du restaurant.

1　Où est la gare?
Opposite the post office and near the coffee shop.

2　Où est la poste?
Opposite the restaurant / opposite the station / next to the pool.

3　Où est la piscine?
Next to the post office.

Write an email to your French penpal telling them about your town.

| Email | To: | aristidep02@speedymail.fr |
| | Subject: | Ma ville |

VARIOUS ANSWERS POSSIBLE

Dans ma ville, il y a une bibliothèque, un café, un restaurant, une piscine et une école. La bibliothèque est en face de l'école. Le café est à côté du restaurant et près de la piscine.

29

As an extension, you could ask your child to draw a map of their town and label it in French.

# Masculine and feminine

All objects in French are either masculine or feminine. This means that the French words for 'the', 'a' and 'my' change depending on whether the word that follows is masculine or feminine.

| feminine | masculine |
|---|---|
| la **chemise** the shirt | le **pull** the jumper |
| une **chemise** a shirt | un **pull** a jumper |
| ma **chemise** my shirt | mon **pull** my jumper |

Fill in the blanks below with either **mon** or **ma**.

Remember
If you're unsure if a word is masculine or feminine, look back through this book.

Mon pull est vert.

Mon pull est violet.

Ma jupe est rose.

Mon tee-shirt est jaune.

Mon chien est marron et blanc.

Mon chat est orange et violet.

Mon chapeau est bleu et ma chemise est verte.

---

Write the French words for the items below on the correct clipboard.

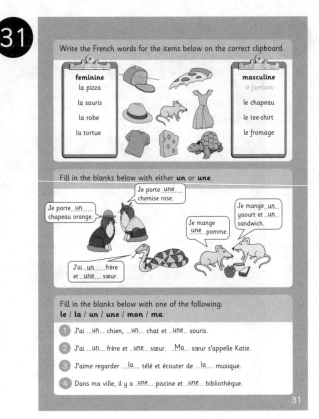

| feminine | masculine |
|---|---|
| la pizza | le jambon |
| la souris | le chapeau |
| la robe | le tee-shirt |
| la tortue | le fromage |

Fill in the blanks below with either **un** or **une**.

Je porte un chapeau orange.

Je porte une chemise rose.

Je mange une pomme.

Je mange un yaourt et un sandwich.

J'ai un frère et une sœur.

Fill in the blanks below with one of the following:
**le / la / un / une / mon / ma**.

1. J'ai un chien, un chat et une souris.

2. J'ai un frère et une sœur. Ma sœur s'appelle Katie.

3. J'aime regarder la télé et écouter de la musique.

4. Dans ma ville, il y a une piscine et une bibliothèque.

You could extend this exercise by asking your child to make lists of the masculine and feminine words in this book.

---

# Plurals

If there's more than one of something, you need to add an 's' to the end of the word (unless there already is an 's').

| une pomme | deux pommes | | une souris | deux souris |
|---|---|---|---|---|
| one apple | two apples | | one mouse | two mice |

| masculine | feminine |
|---|---|
| le **chat** the cat | la **jupe** the skirt |
| les **chat**s the cats | les **jupe**s the skirts |
| mes **chat**s my cats | mes **jupe**s my skirts |
| des **chat**s some cats | des **jupe**s some skirts |

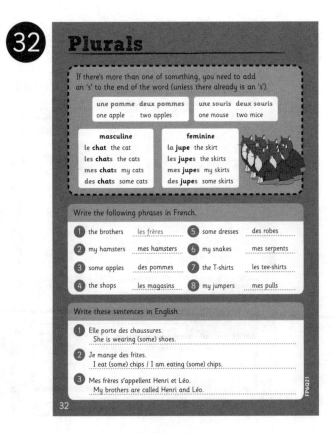

Write the following phrases in French.

| 1 the brothers | les frères | 5 some dresses | des robes |
|---|---|---|---|
| 2 my hamsters | mes hamsters | 6 my snakes | mes serpents |
| 3 some apples | des pommes | 7 the T-shirts | les tee-shirts |
| 4 the shops | les magasins | 8 my jumpers | mes pulls |

Write these sentences in English.

1. Elle porte des chaussures.
   She is wearing (some) shoes.

2. Je mange des frites.
   I eat (some) chips / I am eating (some) chips.

3. Mes frères s'appellent Henri et Léo.
   My brothers are called Henri and Léo.

FP6Q21

**As-tu un animal?**
Do you have a pet?

**Oui, j'ai...**
Yes, I have...

**Non, je n'ai pas d'animaux.**
No, I don't have any pets.

Read the text and answer the questions in English.

> J'ai trois chiens et un chat. Mon chat s'appelle Scruffy et il a deux ans. J'ai quatre lapins et trois araignées.

Karim

1. How many dogs does Karim have? ...........................

2. Karim owns six spiders. True or false? ...........................

3. Who is Scruffy? ...........................

4. How old is Scruffy? ...........................

5. What pet does Karim have four of? ...........................

Your French penpal has sent you an email asking 'As-tu un animal?'. Write your answer below. Give lots of details about your animals.

| Email | To: | aristidep02@speedymail.fr |
|---|---|---|
| | Subject: | Les animaux |

.................................................................................

.................................................................................

.................................................................................

# Clothes
## Les vêtements

le jean

la chemise

le pantalon

le pull

la jupe

le tee-shirt

les chaussettes

les chaussures

la robe

le chapeau

les gants

**Je porte...**
I am wearing...

**Remember!**
In French, the words 'le', 'la' and 'les' all mean 'the'. If you want to say 'a', e.g. 'a dress', you should change 'le' to 'un' and 'la' to 'une'. 'les' changes to 'des' which means 'some'.

Write the English next to each French word.

le pantalon ............................ la jupe ............................

les gants ............................ la robe ............................

la chemise ............................ le jean ............................

Write a sentence in French to say what these characters are wearing.

Je porte un chapeau.

**Il porte...**
He is wearing...

**Elle porte...**
She is wearing...

Circle the sentence that describes each picture best.

Il porte une chemise jaune.

Il porte un chapeau bleu.

Il porte un pull marron.

Elle porte un pantalon rouge.

Il porte une chemise orange.

Il porte un pantalon rouge.

Elle porte une jupe jaune.

Elle porte une robe marron.

Elle porte une robe rose.

Elle porte une robe rose.

Elle porte un tee-shirt rose.

Elle porte un jean rose.

Read the text and answer the questions in English.

Maurice

Je porte un chapeau vert, une chemise jaune et un pantalon bleu. Mon frère s'appelle Clément. Il porte un pull marron et un jean bleu. Ma sœur s'appelle Ella. Elle porte une jupe orange et un tee-shirt violet.

1 Who is wearing a brown jumper? _his brother Clément_

2 What colour are Maurice's trousers? _blue_

3 Who is wearing a purple T-shirt? _his sister Ella_

4 Who is wearing blue jeans? _Clément_

5 What colour is Ella's skirt? _orange_

19

# Food

## La nourriture

le pain  les frites  le sandwich  le jambon  le fromage

la pomme  le chocolat  la pizza  les spaghettis  le yaourt

**Je mange...**
I'm eating...

**Je voudrais...**
I would like...

**Remember!**
In French, the words 'le', 'la' and 'les' all mean 'the'. If you want to say 'some' instead, you should change 'le' to 'du', 'la' to 'de la' and 'les' to 'des', e.g. 'Je mange du pain', 'I am eating some bread'.

Unscramble these French words.

e f e l m
r g a o

j m e l
n b o a

l u e t y
o r a

..........  ..................

..........  ..................

..........  ..................

For each picture, write a sentence to say what you would like.

**Remember!**
If there is more than one of something, add an 's', e.g. 'deux pomme**s**'.

Je voudrais trois pommes.

**la fourchette** the fork
**le couteau** the knife
**la cuillère** the spoon
**l'assiette** the plate

**Peux-tu me passer le couteau, s'il te plaît?**
Can you pass me the knife, please?

Draw lines to match the pictures to the French words.

l'assiette

le couteau

la cuillère

la fourchette

Write these sentences in English.

1 Peux-tu me passer la fourchette, s'il te plaît?

..................................................................................................

2 Je mange du chocolat.

..................................................................................................

3 Peux-tu me passer la cuillère?

..................................................................................................

4 Je voudrais une assiette.

..................................................................................................

21

# What do you like doing?

Qu'est-ce que tu aimes faire?

| J'aime... | Je n'aime pas... |
|---|---|
| I like... | I don't like... |

| ...jouer au foot | ...danser | ...nager | ...jouer du piano |
|---|---|---|---|
| ...playing football | ...dancing | ...swimming | ...playing the piano |

| ...regarder la télé | ...écouter de la musique | ...lire |
|---|---|---|
| ...watching TV | ...listening to music | ...reading |

Write these sentences in English.

J'aime regarder la télé. ➡ ..................................................................

.................................................................. ⬅ Je n'aime pas danser.

J'aime jouer au foot. ➡ ..................................................................

.................................................................. ⬅ Je n'aime pas nager.

Write what each person likes or dislikes doing, in French.

Je n'aime pas lire.

22

Pourquoi?
Why?

Parce que...
Because...

C'est fantastique.
It's fantastic.

C'est intéressant.
It's interesting.

C'est nul.
It's rubbish.

C'est ennuyeux.
It's boring.

## Read the letter and answer the questions in English.

1  Name two things that Agnès likes doing.

.........................................................................

2  What does Agnès say is fantastic?

.........................................................................

3  What does Agnès say is boring?

.........................................................................

4  What does Agnès say is rubbish?

.........................................................................

5  What does Agnès say is interesting?

.........................................................................

J'aime lire, parce que c'est intéressant. J'aime jouer au foot, parce que c'est fantastique.
Je n'aime pas regarder la télé, parce que c'est nul. Je n'aime pas danser, parce que c'est ennuyeux.

Agnès

## Answer the questions below in French.

Qu'est-ce que tu aimes faire?  Pourquoi?

.........................................................................

.........................................................................

23

# What time is it?

## Quelle heure est-il?

| Quelle heure est-il? | À dix heures... | ...du matin |
|---|---|---|
| What time is it? | At ten o'clock... | ...in the morning |
| Il est deux heures... | | ...du soir |
| It's two o'clock... | | ...in the evening |

For each picture below, write down what time it is in French.

Il est une heure.

Monique has written down what she likes doing on a Saturday.
Answer the questions about her routine in English.

À dix heures du matin,
je joue au foot.

À onze heures du matin,
je regarde la télé.

À deux heures, je danse.

À six heures du soir, je joue
du piano.

À huit heures du soir, j'écoute
de la musique.

When does Monique like to dance?

2 o'clock

What does Monique like to do at 11 am?

When does Monique like to play the piano?

What does Monique like to do at 8 pm?

Draw the correct times onto these clocks.

Il est huit heures et quart.

Il est onze heures et demie.

Il est minuit.

Il est trois heures et demie.

Read the question below and give your answer in French.

Quelle heure est-il?

Rewrite these sentences in French.

**Remember!**
Use the words from page 22 to help you answer these questions. In French, words like 'nager' can mean 'to swim' as well as 'swimming'.

1 At midday I like to swim.

   À midi j'aime nager.
......................................................

2 At three o'clock I like to play football.

......................................................

3 At quarter past six in the evening I like to dance.

......................................................

25

# The weather

Le temps

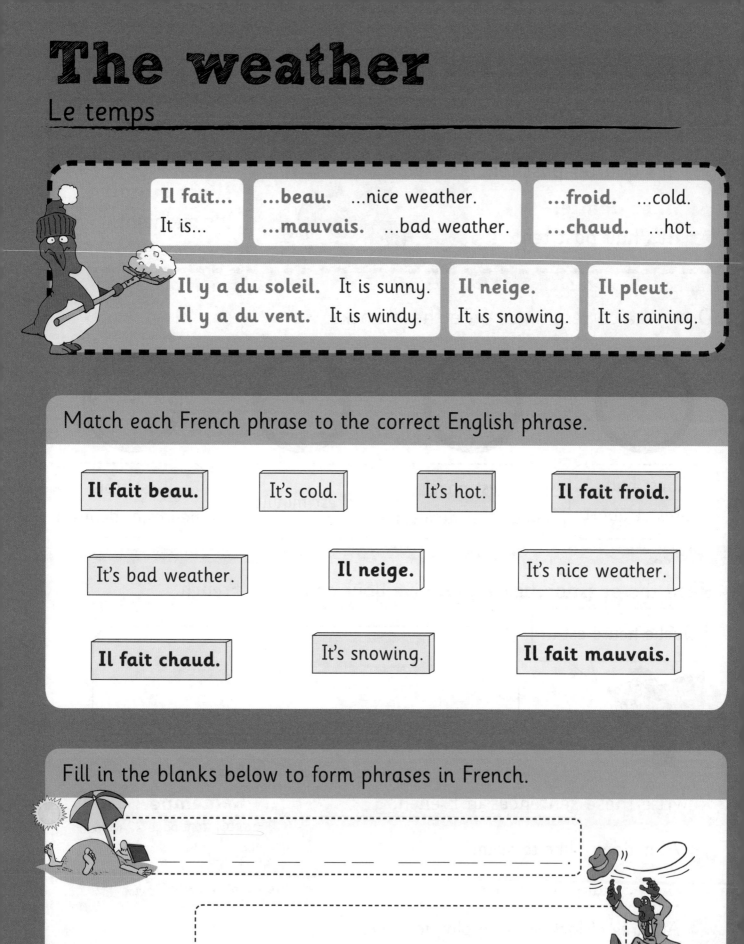

| Il fait... | ...beau. | ...nice weather. | ...froid. | ...cold. |
| It is... | ...mauvais. | ...bad weather. | ...chaud. | ...hot. |

| Il y a du soleil. | It is sunny. | Il neige. | Il pleut. |
| Il y a du vent. | It is windy. | It is snowing. | It is raining. |

Match each French phrase to the correct English phrase.

Il fait beau.    It's cold.    It's hot.    Il fait froid.

It's bad weather.    Il neige.    It's nice weather.

Il fait chaud.    It's snowing.    Il fait mauvais.

Fill in the blanks below to form phrases in French.

**Quel temps fait-il (aujourd'hui)?**   What's the weather like (today)?

Read the question below and give your answer in French.

Quel temps fait-il aujourd'hui?

Write these sentences in French.

1  It is bad weather. ..................................................................................................

2  It is cold. ..................................................................................................

3  It is hot. ..................................................................................................

Claude kept a weather diary for his week in France.  Use it to answer the questions below in English.

| | |
|---|---|
| Mon | Aujourd'hui il fait beau. |
| Tue | Aujourd'hui il fait froid et il pleut. |
| Wed | Aujourd'hui il fait beau. |
| Thu | Aujourd'hui il fait chaud et il y a du vent. |
| Fri | Aujourd'hui il neige. |
| Sat | Aujourd'hui il neige et il y a du vent. |

What was the weather like on Monday?

The weather was nice.
.................................................................

Did it rain on Friday?

.................................................................

What was the weather like on Tuesday?

.................................................................

On which days did it snow?

.................................................................

27

# In my town
## Dans ma ville

l'école
school

la piscine
swimming pool

le café
coffee shop

le restaurant
restaurant

les magasins
shops

la gare
train station

la bibliothèque
library

la poste
post office

**Dans ma ville, il y a...**   In my town, there is / are...

Unscramble these French words.

e s l
a p t o

e i i p l
c s n a

l r u n a e
r s t a e t

........  ................

........  ................

........  ................

**Remember!**
'Il y a' means 'there is' or 'there are'.

Answer the questions below in English.

Leila

Dans ma ville, il y a une gare, une poste, un café, deux écoles, trois piscines, une bibliothèque et des magasins.

1  Is there a restaurant in Leila's town?  ...............................

2  How many coffee shops are there?  ...............................

3  How many swimming pools are there?  ...........................

4  How many schools are there?  .................................................................

5  Is there a library in Leila's town?  .................................................................

| Où est...? | à côté de... | près de... | en face de... |
|---|---|---|---|
| where is...? | next to... | near to... | opposite... |

Answer the questions below in English.

**Remember!**
In French, 'de le' becomes 'du'. So you say 'en face du restaurant', not 'en face de le restaurant'.

La piscine est à côté de la poste. La gare est en face de la poste et près du café.

Le café est à côté de la gare et en face de l'école. La poste est en face du restaurant.

1 Où est la gare?

...... Opposite the post office and near the coffee shop. ......

2 Où est la poste?

......................................................................................

3 Où est la piscine?

......................................................................................

Write an email to your French penpal telling them about your town.

| Email | To: | aristidep02@speedymail.fr |
|---|---|---|
| | Subject: | Ma ville |

......................................................................................

......................................................................................

Où est......................... à côté de......................... près de......................... en face de.........

29

# Masculine and feminine

All objects in French are either masculine or feminine. This means that the French words for 'the', 'a' and 'my' change depending on whether the word that follows is masculine or feminine.

**feminine**
la **chemise** the shirt
une **chemise** a shirt
ma **chemise** my shirt

**masculine**
le **pull** the jumper
un **pull** a jumper
mon **pull** my jumper

Fill in the blanks below with either **mon** or **ma**.

Remember! If you're unsure if a word is masculine or feminine, look back through this book.

............ pull est violet.

.Mon.... pull est vert.

............jupe est rose.

............tee-shir est jaune.

.......... chien est marron et blanc.

.......... chapeau est bleu et ..........chemise est verte.

.......... chat est orange et violet.

Write the French words for the items below on the correct clipboard.

**feminine**

**masculine**
le jambon

Fill in the blanks below with either **un** or **une**.

Je porte.............
chemise rose.

e porte.............
hapeau orange.

J'ai.............frère
et ............. sœur.

Je mange
......... pomme.

Je mange.........
yaourt et .........
sandwich.

Fill in the blanks below with one of the following:
**le / la / un / une / mon / ma**.

1  J'ai ......... chien, ......... chat et ......... souris.

2  J'ai ......... frère et ......... sœur.  ......... sœur s'appelle Katie.

3  J'aime regarder ......... télé et écouter de ......... musique.

4  Dans ma ville, il y a ......... piscine et ......... bibliothèque.

31

# Plurals

If there's more than one of something, you need to add an 's' to the end of the word (unless there already is an 's').

| une pomme | deux pommes |
|-----------|-------------|
| one apple | two apples  |

| une souris | deux souris |
|------------|-------------|
| one mouse  | two mice    |

**masculine**

le **chat**  the cat

les **chats**  the cats

mes **chats**  my cats

des **chats**  some cats

**feminine**

la **jupe**  the skirt

les **jupes**  the skirts

mes **jupes**  my skirts

des **jupes**  some skirts

Write the following phrases in French.

1 the brothers  *les frères*

2 my hamsters  ............................

3 some apples  ............................

4 the shops  ............................

5 some dresses  ............................

6 my snakes  ............................

7 the T-shirts  ............................

8 my jumpers  ............................

Write these sentences in English.

1 Elle porte des chaussures.

............................................................

2 Je mange des frites.

............................................................

3 Mes frères s'appellent Henri et Léo.

............................................................